Gluten-Free Slow Cooker Cookbook

40 Dairy Free Crock Pot Recipes to Reduce Gluten Intolerance Symptoms

By Kira Novac (ISBN-13: 978-1533622723)

Copyright ©Kira Novac 2016

www.amazon.com/author/kira-novac

Free Complimentary Recipe eBook

Thank you so much for taking an interest in my work!

As a thank you, I would love to offer you a free complimentary recipe eBook to help you achieve vibrant health. It will teach you how to prepare amazingly tasty and healthy gluten-free treats so that you never feel deprived or bored again!

As a special bonus, you will be able to receive all my future books (kindle format) for free or only $0.99.

Download your free recipe eBook here:

http://bit.ly/gluten-free-desserts-book

GLUTEN-FREE, GUILT-FREE AND STRESS-FREE!

GLUTEN-FREE, GUILT-FREE AND STRESS-FREE!

Irresistible Glu
Snacks and Treats
Weight Loss and

(PALEO AND VEGAN OP

KIRA NOVAC

FREE GIFT
★ LIMITED OFFER ★

Table of contents

Introduction

Every year more and more people switch to the gluten-free diet. While many people do so simply as a matter of preference, there are those for whom it is a medical necessity. Gluten sensitivities and intolerances are becoming increasingly more common, as is Celiac disease – this is an autoimmune disease triggered by the consumption of gluten. No matter what your reasoning for switching to the gluten-free diet, you will be glad to know that making the switch won't require you to completely give up all of your favorite foods. In this book you will find a collection of delicious gluten-free recipes such as breakfast casseroles, soups, stews, main entrees, snacks, and desserts.

All of the recipes in this book are completely gluten-free and many of them are compatibility with other diets like the Paleo diet as well as the vegan and vegetarian diets. As an added bonus, they are all incredibly easy to prepare because they are designed for the slow cooker! The slow cooker may be one of the most essential and versatile kitchen appliances out there – you can use it to create everything from your morning oatmeal to a delicious dinner for four, all with minimal preparation time. So, if you are ready to give the gluten-free diet a try and you want to test out your slow cooker, this book is the perfect place to start! Just turn the page and keep reading!

PART 1

Gluten-Free Slow Cooker Breakfast Recipes

Paleo Crustless Spinach Tomato Quiche

Servings: 6

Ingredients:

- Cooking spray
- 10 ounces of frozen spinach (1 package), thawed
- 2 vine-ripened tomatoes, cored and chopped up
- 1 medium yellow onion, chopped up
- 2 cloves of garlic, minced
- 10 large eggs, beaten well

- ¼ cup of unsweetened almond milk
- Salt and pepper to taste

Instructions:

1. Lightly spray the insert of your slow cooker using cooking spray to keep the egg from sticking to the sides.
2. Put the frozen spinach in a colander and press it down by hand to get rid of as much water as you can.
3. Combine your chopped tomatoes and onions in your slow cooker then stir in your garlic and the drained spinach.
4. In a mixing bowl, whisk together your eggs and almond milk – season with salt and pepper to taste.
5. Pour the mixture into your slow cooker then cover it with the lid.
6. Let your quiche cook for 7 to 8 hours on the low heat setting until the middle is set.
7. Take the lid off the slow cooker and let your quiche cool for 10 to 15 minutes before you cut it and serve it up hot.

Blueberry Quinoa and Oats Breakfast
Servings: 6 to 8

Ingredients:

- 1 ½ cups of steel-cut oats
- ½ cup of uncooked quinoa
- 4 ½ cups of fat-free milk or water
- ¼ cup of light brown sugar
- 2 tablespoons of honey
- 2 teaspoons of vanilla extract
- ½ teaspoon of ground cinnamon
- Pinch of salt
- 1 to 2 cups of fresh blueberries

Instructions:

1. Spray the inside of your slow cooker with cooking spray so the ingredients don't stick.
2. Rinse your quinoa with cold water several times until the water runs clear.

3.   Pour the quinoa into your slow cooker and add in your oats and the rest of the ingredients except for the blueberries.

4.   Give your ingredients a good stir and then cover the slow cooker with the lid.

5.   Let your quinoa and oats cook on the low heat setting for about 6 to 7 hours.

6.   Turn off the slow cooker and then spoon the mixture into bowls.

7.   Sprinkle fresh blueberries on the quinoa and oats to serve it.

Paleo Spiced Pumpkin Butter Spread
Servings: 10 to 12

Ingredients:

- 2 (15-ounce) cans of pure pumpkin
- 1 ½ cups of pure maple syrup
- 1 tablespoon of ground cinnamon
- ½ teaspoon of ground nutmeg
- 1 ½ teaspoons of vanilla extract
- Pinch of salt

Instructions:

1. Spray the inside of your slow cooker with cooking spray so the ingredients don't stick.
2. Empty your cans of pumpkin into the slow cooker then pour in the maple syrup.
3. Add in the cinnamon and nutmeg as well as the vanilla and salt.
4. Stir everything together very well and then put the lid on the slow cooker.
5. Let your pumpkin butter cook for 7 to 8 hours on the low heat setting.
6. If you want your pumpkin butter to be thicker, crack the lid a little bit during the last hour of cook time.
7. Let your pumpkin butter cool then spoon it into jars and store it.

Vegan Sweet Potato, Carrot and Mushroom Hash

Servings: 10 to 12

Ingredients:

- 1 tablespoon of coconut oil
- 2 lbs. of sweet potatoes, peeled and chopped up
- 1 pound of carrots, peeled and sliced
- 8 ounces of sliced white mushrooms
- 1 small yellow onion, chopped up
- 1 clove of garlic minced
- 2 cups of vegetable broth, low-sodium
- 2 tablespoons of cornstarch
- 1 teaspoon of fresh rosemary, chopped
- 1 teaspoon of fresh thyme, chopped
- Pepper and salt to taste
- Toasted walnuts, optional

Instructions:

1. Heat up the coconut oil in a large skillet on the medium-high heat setting.

2.   Add your sweet potatoes and sauté them for about 5 minutes until they are lightly browned.

3.   Spoon your sautéed sweet potatoes into your slow cooker and add in your carrots, mushrooms, onions, and the garlic.

4.   In a mixing bowl, whisk your vegetable broth together with your cornstarch and the herbs – season it with pepper and salt to taste.

5.   Pour the liquid mixture into your slow cooker and stir the ingredients together a little bit.

6.   Cover your slow cooker and let the hash cook for 8 to 9 hours until the vegetables are tender.

7.   Serve your sweet potato hash hot and sprinkle with toasted walnuts, if you like.

Apple Cranberry Slow Cooker Oatmeal
Servings: 6 to 8

Ingredients:

- Cooking spray
- 6 cups of water
- 3 cups of old-fashioned oats (gluten-free)
- 2 medium ripe apples, peeled, cored and chopped up
- ½ cup to ¾ cups of dried cranberries
- 1 teaspoon of ground cinnamon
- Pinch of salt
- 2 tablespoons of unsalted butter, melted

Instructions:

1. Lightly grease your slow cooker using cooking spray to prevent the oatmeal from sticking.
2. Pour the water into the slow cooker along with your oats.
3. Sprinkle the apples and cranberries over the oats and then stir in your cinnamon and the salt.

4.   Pour in the melted butter and then stir it all together very well.

5.   Cover your slow cooker and cook the oatmeal on low heat for about 6 to 8 hours.

6.   Spoon your oatmeal into bowls to serve and drizzle them with honey or maple syrup.

Vegetarian Spinach, Mushroom, and Onion Casserole

Servings: 6 to 8

Ingredients:

- Cooking spray
- 10 ounces of frozen spinach (1 package), thawed
- 8 ounces of sliced mushrooms
- 1 medium yellow onion, chopped up
- 1 medium red pepper, cored and chopped up
- 1 clove of garlic, minced
- 10 large eggs, beaten well
- ¼ cup of coconut milk
- Salt and pepper to taste

Instructions:

1. Lightly spray the insert of your slow cooker using cooking spray to keep the egg from sticking to the sides.
2. Put the frozen spinach in a colander and press it down by hand to get rid of as much water as you can.

3.   Chop the sliced mushrooms a little bit then pour them into the slow cooker with your onions and red peppers.

4.   Add your garlic and the drained spinach to the mixture.

5.   In a mixing bowl, whisk together your eggs and coconut milk – season with salt and pepper to taste.

6.   Pour the mixture into your slow cooker then cover it with the lid.

7.   Let your casserole cook for 7 to 8 hours on the low heat setting until the middle is set.

8.   Take the lid off the slow cooker and let your casserole cool for 10 to 15 minutes before you cut it and serve it up hot.

Paleo Herbed Broccoli and Onion Frittata
Servings: 6

Ingredients:

- 2 cups of fresh chopped broccoli florets
- 8 ounces of sliced white mushrooms
- 1 large yellow onion, chopped up
- 12 large eggs, whisked well
- 1 cup of unsweetened almond milk

- 2 teaspoons of assorted dried herbs
- Pepper and salt to taste

Instructions:

1. Place your broccoli, mushrooms and onions in your slow cooker and stir them together.
2. In a mixing bowl, whisk up your eggs with the almond milk and herbs.
3. Season that mixture with pepper and salt according to your taste and pour it into the slow cooker.
4. Cover your slow cooker and let the frittata cook for 7 to 8 hours until the middle is set.
5. Take off the lid and let the frittata cool for 10 to 15 minutes then slice it up to serve.

Red Pepper and Sweet Potato Hash
Servings: 6 to 8

Ingredients:

- 2 teaspoons of olive oil
- 1 lbs. of sweet potatoes, peeled and chopped up
- 1 medium red pepper, cored and chopped up
- 1 cup of fresh chopped cauliflower florets
- 1 small yellow onion, chopped up
- 1 clove of garlic minced
- 1 cup of vegetable broth, low-sodium

- 1 tablespoon of cornstarch
- 2 to 3 sprigs of fresh herbs (rosemary, thyme, etc.)
- Pepper and salt to taste

Instructions:

1. Heat up the olive oil in a large skillet on the medium-high heat setting.
2. Add your sweet potatoes and red peppers then sauté them for about 5 minutes until the sweet potatoes are lightly browned.
3. Spoon your sautéed sweet potatoes into your slow cooker and add in your cauliflower, onions, and the garlic.
4. In a mixing bowl, whisk your vegetable broth together with your cornstarch – season it with pepper and salt to taste.
5. Pour the liquid mixture into your slow cooker and stir the ingredients together a little bit.
6. Place the sprigs of fresh herbs on top of the vegetable mixture.
7. Cover your slow cooker and let the hash cook for 8 to 9 hours until the vegetables are tender.
8. Discard the sprigs of herbs and then serve your sweet potato hash hot.

Mediterranean-Style Breakfast Casserole

Servings: 6 to 8

Ingredients:

- Cooking spray
- 10 ounces of frozen spinach (1 package), thawed
- 2 vine-ripened tomatoes, cored and chopped up
- 1 small red onion, chopped up
- ¼ cup of sliced black olives
- 1 clove of garlic, minced
- ½ cup of crumbled feta cheese
- 10 large eggs, beaten well
- ¼ cup of milk
- Salt and pepper to taste

Instructions:

1. Lightly spray the insert of your slow cooker using cooking spray to keep the egg from sticking to the sides.
2. Put the frozen spinach in a colander and press it down by hand to get rid of as much water as you can.

3.   Combine your red pepper and chopped tomatoes with the onions and olives in your slow cooker.

4.   Stir in your garlic and the drained spinach then sprinkle on your feta cheese.

5.   In a mixing bowl, whisk together your eggs and your milk – season with salt and pepper to taste.

6.   Pour the mixture into your slow cooker then cover it with the lid.

7.   Let your casserole cook for 7 to 8 hours on the low heat setting until the middle is set.

8.   Take the lid off the slow cooker and let your casserole cool for 10 to 15 minutes before you cut it and serve it up hot.

Cinnamon Raisin Slow Cooker Oatmeal
Servings: 6 to 8

Ingredients:

- Cooking spray
- 8 cups of water
- 2 cups of steel-cut oats, uncooked
- 2 cups of milk (whole or 2% is best)
- 4 tablespoons of light brown sugar
- 1 ½ teaspoons of ground cinnamon
- 1 teaspoon of vanilla extract
- Pinch of salt

Instructions:

1. Lightly grease your slow cooker using cooking spray to prevent the oatmeal from sticking.
2. Pour the water into the slow cooker along with your steel-cut oats.
3. Stir in your milk and brown sugar along with the cinnamon, vanilla extract and the salt.

4.   Cover your slow cooker and cook the oatmeal on low heat for about 6 to 8 hours.

5.   Stir in your raisins and then cook for another 30 minutes or so.

6.   Spoon your oatmeal into bowls to serve and drizzle them with honey or maple syrup.

Vegan Cinnamon Spiced Apple Butter Spread

Servings: 10 to 12

Ingredients:

- 5 pounds of ripe apples
- ½ cup of unsweetened apple juice
- 1 tablespoon of ground cinnamon
- 1 tablespoon of lemon juice
- Honey, if desired

Instructions:

1.   Spray the inside of your slow cooker with cooking spray so the ingredients don't stick.

2.   Slice up your apples nice and thin and then put them in your slow cooker with the apple juice.

3.   Put the lid on the slow cooker and let your apples cook for about 4 hours on the high heat setting.

4.   Turn the slow cooker off and mash up the apples using a potato masher.

5.   Let the mashed apples cool a little bit and then transfer them to a blender.

6.   Blend the apple mixture until it is very smooth and then pour it back into your slow cooker.

7.   Let your apple mixture butter cook for another 60 to 90 minutes with the lid off on the high heat setting until it is thickened.

8.   Stir in your cinnamon and lemon juice – add honey to sweeten if you want.

9.   Let your apple butter cool then spoon it into jars and store it.

PART 2

Gluten-Free Slow Cooker Soups and Stews

Vegetarian Black Bean Chili
Servings: 8 to 10

Ingredients:

- 1 pound of dried black beans, rinsed well
- 1 large onion, chopped or sliced
- 4 tablespoons of chili powder
- 1 teaspoon of ground cumin
- ½ teaspoon of garlic powder
- Pepper and salt to taste
- 2 (15-ounce) cans of roasted diced tomatoes
- 6 tablespoons of tomato paste
- 3 cups of water
- Diced red onion, to serve
- Chopped cilantro, to serve

Instructions:

1. Pour the black beans into your slow cooker and then add the onions on top.

2.   Sprinkle in the chili powder, cumin, and garlic powder then season with pepper and salt according to your tastes.

3.   Pour in your diced tomatoes along with the tomato paste and then add the water.

4.   Stir all of the ingredients together very well and then place the lid on the slow cooker.

5.   Let everything cook on the low heat setting for 6 to 8 hours until the beans are tender.

6.   Serve the chili hot with diced red onion and fresh chopped cilantro.

Cheesy Chicken Enchilada Soup
Servings: 6 to 8

Ingredients:

- 2 (15-ounce) cans of black beans, rinsed and drained
- 1 (15-ounce) can of roasted diced tomatoes, undrained
- 1 (15-ounce) can of whole kernel corn, drained
- 1 large yellow onion, sliced thin
- ½ cup of diced green chilies
- 1 ½ pounds of boneless skinless chicken breasts
- 2 ½ cups of chicken stock
- 1 (10-ounce) can of enchilada sauce
- 1 ¼ teaspoons of ground cumin
- Pepper and salt to taste
- 1 cup of shredded cheddar cheese

Instructions:

1. Combine your beans, tomatoes and corn in the bottom of your slow cooker.
2. Place the onions, chilies and the chicken breasts on top of this mixture.

3. Stir together your chicken stock along with the enchilada sauce and cumin then season with pepper and salt to taste.

4. Pour the liquid into your slow cooker and then cover it with the lid.

5. Let everything cook for 6 to 8 hours on the low heat setting until the chicken is done.

6. Shred the chicken and stir everything together very well.

7. Stir the cheese into the soup just before serving then spoon it into bowls and serve hot.

Vegetarian Lentil Split Pea Soup
Servings: 10 to 12

Ingredients:

- 1 lbs. dried split peas
- 1 lbs. dried green lentils
- 12 cups of low-sodium vegetable broth
- 4 large carrots, peeled and chopped
- 1 large yellow onion, chopped
- 2 medium stalks celery, chopped

- 3 cloves of minced garlic
- Pepper and salt to taste
- 1 ½ teaspoons of Italian seasoning blend

Instructions:

1. Rinse your split peas and dried lentils well and then combine them in your slow cooker.
2. Pour in the chicken broth and then add the carrots, onions, celery and garlic.
3. Season everything with pepper and salt to taste then sprinkle with Italian seasoning.
4. Cover your slow cooker and let everything cook for 7 to 8 hours on the low heat setting.
5. When the beans and lentils are tender, use an immersion blender to puree some of the soup mixture.
6. Adjust the seasonings if needed and then spoon everything into bowls and serve hot.

Paleo Tomato Basil Soup

Servings: 6 to 8

Ingredients:

- 2 (15-ounce) cans of roasted diced tomatoes
- 1 ½ cups of plain tomato sauce
- 1 large yellow onion, chopped up
- 2 cloves of minced garlic
- ¼ cup of fresh chopped basil leaves
- Pepper and salt to taste

- 4 ½ cups of vegetable broth
- 1 (15-ounce) can of coconut milk

Instructions:

1. Pour your diced tomatoes and tomato sauce into the slow cooker.
2. Add the onions, garlic and basil on top then season with pepper and salt according to your taste.
3. Stir in your vegetable broth and then cover the slow cooker with the lid.
4. Let everything cook for 6 to 8 hours on the low heat setting, stirring occasionally.
5. Turn off the slow cooker and puree everything together using an immersion blender.
6. Stir in the coconut milk and then adjust the seasonings to taste.
7. Heat the soup for another 15 minutes, if needed, and then spoon into bowls to serve.

Vegan Curried Chickpea Vegetable Stew

Servings: 8 to 10

Ingredients:

- 1 teaspoon of olive oil
- 2 medium yellow onions, chopped
- 1 tablespoon of minced garlic
- 2 medium Yukon gold potatoes, peeled and chopped
- 2 cups of low-sodium vegetable broth
- 2 (15-ounce) cans of chickpeas, rinsed and drained

- 2 (14-ounce) cans of diced tomatoes, undrained
- 1 head of cauliflower, chopped up
- 2 assorted bell peppers, cored and chopped
- 1 carrot, peeled and sliced or chopped
- Pepper and salt to taste
- 1 cup of canned coconut milk
- 10 ounces of fresh baby spinach, chopped

Instructions:

1. Heat the oil in a large skillet on the medium heat setting until hot.
2. Add the onions and garlic and sauté them for 4 to 5 minutes until just tender.
3. Put the potatoes in the skillet with the onions and cook them until they are just browned.
4. Transfer this mixture to your slow cooker and pour in the vegetable broth.
5. Add in the chickpeas, diced tomatoes, and vegetables then season everything with pepper and salt to taste.
6. Stir it all up, adding more broth if needed, then cover the slow cooker.
7. Let everything cook for about 4 hours on the high heat setting.

8.   Stir in your coconut milk and the spinach then cover the slow cooker and let rest for 5 minutes.

9.   Adjust the seasonings to taste and then serve the stew hot.

Spicy Green Chicken Chili
Servings: 8 to 10

Ingredients:

- 2 large yellow onions, chopped
- 2 medium green bell peppers, chopped
- 2 large jalapenos, seeded and sliced thin
- ½ cup of canned green chilies
- 4 chicken breast halves, boneless and skinless
- 4 cups of prepared salsa verde
- 2 (15-ounce) cans of white cannellini or navy beans
- 1 cup of sour cream
- ½ cup of fresh chopped cilantro

Instructions:

1. Combine your onions, green peppers, jalapenos, and the chilis in your slow cooker.
2. Place the chicken breast halves on top of the vegetables and then pour the *salsa verde* over everything.
3. Cover your slow cooker and let everything cook for 5 to 6 hours on the low heat setting.

4.   When the chicken is cooked through remove it from the slow cooker and shred it up before stirring it back in.

5.   Add in the beans, sour cream, and the cilantro and let everything cook for another 15 minutes or so.

6.   Spoon your chili into bowls and serve sprinkled with cheese, if desired.

Vegan Pumpkin Butternut Squash Soup
Servings: 6 to 8

Ingredients:

- 1 medium butternut squash
- 1 medium yellow onion, chopped up
- 1 small Granny Smith apple, peeled, cored and chopped
- 1 large carrot, peeled and chopped up
- 2 cloves of garlic, minced
- 2 1/2 cups of vegetable stock
- ½ teaspoon dried sage
- ¼ teaspoon of ground cinnamon
- Pepper and salt to taste
- 1 (15-ounce) can of pumpkin puree
- 1 cup of unsweetened almond milk

Instructions:

1. Cut your butternut squash in half lengthwise and then scoop out and discard the seeds.
2. Peel away the flesh with a sharp knife and cut the squash into cubes – place them in the slow cooker.

3. Add the onions, apple, carrot, and garlic to your slow cooker.

4. Stir together your vegetable stock with the sage, cinnamon, pepper and salt then pour it into the slow cooker.

5. Cover your slow cooker and let everything cook for 6 to 8 hours on the low heat setting.

6. Turn off the slow cooker and use an immersion blender to puree everything.

7. Stir in your pumpkin puree along with your almond milk until thoroughly blended.

8. Turn the slow cooker back on and let everything cook for 20 minutes or so until it is heated through then adjust the seasonings if needed.

Paleo Beef and Root Vegetable Stew
Servings: 6 to 8

Ingredients:

- 1 tablespoon olive oil
- 2 pounds of boneless chuck roast, cut into cubes
- Pepper and salt to taste
- 2 large yellow onions, sliced thick
- 1 ½ tablespoons of minced garlic
- 1 pound of sweet potatoes, peeled and cubed

- 1 pound of carrots, peeled and sliced
- ½ pound of turnips, peeled and sliced
- 3 cups of beef stock
- 2 medium bay leaves
- 3 sprigs of fresh thyme
- 1 tablespoon of arrowroot powder

Instructions:

1. Heat a large skillet on the medium-high heat setting and add the oil.
2. Let the oil heat up while you season the beef with pepper and salt to taste.
3. Add the beef to the skillet and cook it for a few minutes on each side until it is browned.
4. Remove the beef from the skillet and reheat it then add the onions and garlic – cook them for 3 to 4 minutes until softened.
5. Transfer the onions to the slow cooker along with the browned beef, the vegetables, the herbs, and the beef stock.
6. Cover your slow cooker and let everything cook for 7 hours on the low heat setting.
7. At the end, spoon out ¼ cup of the cooking liquid and whisk in the arrowroot powder to create a slurry.

8.   Stir the slurry back into the slow cooker and cook it for 15 minutes until the gravy thickens.

9.   Spoon everything into bowls and serve hot.

Cheesy Potato Corn Chowder
Servings: 8 to 10

Ingredients:

- 4 slices of bacon, uncooked
- 1 medium yellow onion, chopped up
- 3 pounds of russet potatoes, peeled and sliced ¼ inch thick
- ½ cup of water
- 3 ½ cups of chicken broth

- Pepper and salt to taste

- 2 cups of nonfat milk

- 1 ½ cups of frozen corn kernels

- 1 cup of shredded cheddar cheese

Instructions:

1. Cook your bacon in a nonstick skillet until it is crisp and then let it drain on paper towels.

2. Remove all but 1 tablespoon of the bacon fat from the skillet and then reheat it on the medium heat setting.

3. Add the onions and cook for 3 to 4 minutes until they are tender.

4. Place your sliced potatoes in the slow cooker with the onions after spraying it with cooking spray.

5. Stir together the water with the chicken broth, pepper and salt and then pour it into the slow cooker.

6. Cover your slow cooker and let everything cook for 8 hours on the low heat setting.

7. Remove the lid and then use a potato masher to mash the ingredients together then stir in your milk, corn, and cheese.

8. Cover your slow cooker once more and let everything cook for 20 minutes on high heat.

9.   Spoon the soup into bowl and serve with the crumbled bacon.

Easy French Onion Soup
Servings: 10 to 12

Ingredients:

- 4 tablespoons of unsalted butter
- 1 large bay leaf
- 4 to 5 sprigs of fresh thyme
- 4 ½ to 5 pounds of yellow onion, sliced
- 2 teaspoons of white granulated sugar
- 6 cups of beef broth

- 2 tablespoons of red wine vinegar
- Pepper and salt to taste
- Toasted baguette slices, to serve
- Cheese, to serve

Instructions:

1. Put your butter in the bottom of your slow cooker along with the bay leaf and thyme.
2. Sprinkle the onions and the sugar into the slow cooker then cover it with the lid.
3. Let the onions cook for about 8 hours on the high heat setting then discard the bay leaf and the thyme.
4. Pour in the beef broth and vinegar then season it with pepper and salt to taste.
5. Cover the slow cooker again and cook the mixture on high for 30 minutes.
6. Serve the soup hot with toasted baguette slices and melted cheese.

PART 3

Gluten-Free Slow Cooker Entrees

Spicy Chicken Vegetable Fajitas
Servings: 4

Ingredients:

- 1 (15-ounce) can of diced tomatoes with green chilies
- 1 large yellow onion, sliced up
- 3 assorted bell peppers, cored and sliced
- 2 jalapeno peppers, cored and sliced thin
- 2 pounds of boneless skinless chicken breast
- 3 cloves of minced garlic

- 1 tablespoon of chili powder
- 2 teaspoons of ground cumin
- 1 teaspoon of paprika
- ½ teaspoon of dried coriander
- ¼ teaspoon of cayenne
- Pepper and salt to taste
- Warmed corn tortillas

Instructions:

1. Empty the can of tomatoes into the bottom of your slow cooker and spread it around.
2. Place half of the onions and peppers on top of the tomatoes then add the chicken and garlic on top of that.
3. Stir together your chili powder, cumin, paprika, coriander, and cayenne in a small bowl and add pepper and salt to taste.
4. Sprinkle half of this mixture over the chicken and then add the rest of the peppers and onions along with the jalapenos.
5. Add the rest of the spice mixture to the slow cooker and then cover it with the lid.
6. Let everything cook for 6 to 8 hours on the low heat setting until the chicken is done.

7.   Remove and slice the chicken then use a slotted spoon to remove the peppers and onions to a serving dish.

8.   Prepare your fajitas using warmed corn tortillas and serve hot.

Vegan Sweet Potatoes with Lentils
Servings: 6 to 8

Ingredients:

- 6 cups of chopped sweet potatoes
- 1 large yellow onion, chopped
- 3 cloves of minced garlic
- 3 cups of low-sodium vegetable broth
- 2 teaspoons of dried coriander
- 2 teaspoons of chili powder
- 1 teaspoon of ground turmeric
- Pepper and salt to taste
- 1 (15-ounce) can of red lentils
- 1 (15-ounce) can of coconut milk
- ½ cup of water

Instructions:

1. Spread your chopped sweet potatoes in the bottom of your slow cooker.
2. Add the onions and garlic then pour in the vegetable broth.

53

3.   Sprinkle in the coriander, chili powder, and turmeric and then season it all with pepper and salt to taste.

4.   Cover your slow cooker with the lid and let everything cook for 3 hours on the high heat setting.

5.   Stir in your lentils and then cook for another hour and a half.

6.   Add in the coconut milk and water then cook for 20 minutes until heated through before serving.

Barbecue Pulled Pork for Sandwiches
Servings: 6 to 8

Ingredients:

- ¼ cup of brown sugar, packed
- 1 ¼ teaspoons of chili powder
- ½ teaspoon of garlic powder
- Pepper and salt to taste
- 2 pounds of boneless pork shoulder
- ½ cup of water

- ½ cup of apple cider vinegar
- 1 cup of barbecue sauce

Instructions:

1. Combine your brown sugar, chili powder, and garlic powder in a small bowl.
2. Season your pork with pepper and salt to taste and then rub the sugar mixture all over it before putting it in the slow cooker.
3. Pour in the water and the apple cider vinegar and then cover the slow cooker with the lid.
4. Cook the pork for about 7 to 8 hours on low heat until it is very tender.
5. Remove the pork to a bowl and then shred it using two forks.
6. Stir in the barbecue sauce and then serve the pork hot on toasted gluten-free sandwich buns.

Paleo Beef with Broccoli
Servings: 6 to 8

Ingredients:

- 1 ½ cups of low-sodium beef broth
- ¾ cups of coconut aminos
- ½ cup of raw honey
- 1 tablespoon of sesame oil
- 1 tablespoon of minced garlic
- 1 ½ pounds of boneless beef chuck, sliced thin
- 1 tablespoon of arrowroot powder
- 4 cups of frozen broccoli florets

Instructions:

1. Whisk together your beef broth, coconut aminos, honey, sesame oil, and minced garlic in a small bowl then pour it into your slow cooker.
2. Add the beef to the slow cooker and toss it in the sauce.
3. Cover your slow cooker with the lid and cook for 6 hours on the low heat setting.

4.   When the beef is cooked through, whisk together ½ cup of the cooking liquid with the arrowroot powder to create a slurry.

5.   Stir the slurry and the broccoli florets into the slow cooker and cover it again.

6.   Cook for 30 minutes on the low heat setting until heated through.

7.   Serve the beef with broccoli over cauliflower rice for a Paleo option or steamed brown rice for a non-Paleo option.

Chicken Tikka Masala with Cucumber Slaw

Servings: 6 to 8

Ingredients:

- 2 (14.5-ounce) cans of crushed tomatoes
- 1 large yellow onion, chopped
- 4 cloves of minced garlic
- 2 ½ pounds of boneless skinless chicken breast
- ¼ cup of tomato paste
- 1 tablespoon of garam masala
- Pepper and salt to taste
- 1 English cucumber, sliced thin
- ½ cup of fresh chopped cilantro
- 2 tablespoons of fresh lemon juice
- Steamed rice, to serve

Instructions:

1. Empty the can of tomatoes into your slow cooker and then add your onions and garlic.

2.   In a small bowl, whisk together your tomato paste with the garam masala then season it with pepper and salt to taste.

3.   Place the chicken on top of the vegetables in the slow cooker and spoon the sauce over top.

4.   Cover the slow cooker with the lid and let everything cook for 7 to 8 hours on low heat.

5.   In a bowl, toss together the sliced cucumber with the cilantro and lemon juice then refrigerate until the chicken is done.

6.   Stir the cream into the chicken tikka masala once it is cooked and then serve it on steamed rice with the cucumber slaw.

Gluten-Free Spaghetti with Bolognese Sauce

Servings: 6 to 8

Ingredients:

- 1 ½ pounds of lean ground beef
- 3 (14-ounce) cans of crushed tomatoes
- 3 medium carrots, peeled and diced up
- 1 large yellow onion, chopped up

- 1 medium stalk celery, chopped
- 1 tablespoon of minced garlic
- 6 tablespoons of tomato paste
- 1/3 cup of dry white wine
- 1 ½ teaspoons of dried oregano
- 1 ½ teaspoons of dried thyme
- Pepper and salt to taste
- 2 small bay leaves
- 1 pound of gluten-free spaghetti

Instructions:

1. Combine your beef and tomatoes in the bottom of your slow cooker then add the carrots, onion, celery and garlic.
2. Whisk together your tomato paste and white wine with the oregano, and thyme then season it with pepper and salt to taste.
3. Pour this mixture into the slow cooker and add the bay leaf.
4. Cover the slow cooker and let everything cook for 7 to 8 hours until the beef is cooked through.
5. During the last 20 minutes of cooking, bring a large pot of salted water to boil.

6.   Add the spaghetti and cook to al dente according to the directions, about 9 to 15 minutes.

7.   Drain the pasta and stir it into the sauce in the slow cooker then serve hot.

Easy Homemade Pot Roast
Servings: 6 to 8

Ingredients:

- 1 cup of water
- ¼ cup of tomato paste
- 2 tablespoons of cornstarch
- 1 pound of Yukon gold potatoes, peeled and quartered
- 1 pound of carrots, peeled and sliced thick
- 1 large yellow onion, chopped

- 1 large stalk of celery, sliced
- 1 bay leaf
- 3 ½ pounds of boneless beef chuck roast
- Pepper and salt to taste

Instructions:

1. Whisk together your water, tomato paste, and cornstarch in a bowl then pour it into your slow cooker.
2. Add in the potatoes, carrots, onion and celery, tossing it all together, then place the bay leaf on top.
3. Season the beef according to your taste with pepper and salt and then place it in the slow cooker.
4. Cover your slow cooker and let everything cook for 7 to 8 hours on low heat.
5. When the beef is done, remove it to a cutting board and let it rest for 10 minutes before slicing it.
6. Serve the sliced beef with the vegetables and cooking liquid.

Chicken with Bacon and Mushrooms

Servings: 6 to 8

Ingredients:

- ½ to ¾ pounds of uncooked bacon, diced up
- 1 (5 to 6 pound) chicken, cut into pieces
- ½ cup of dry white wine
- 10 ounces sliced white mushrooms
- 1 large yellow onion, chopped
- 1 ½ tablespoons of fresh minced garlic
- 1 tablespoon of dried rosemary
- 1 teaspoon of dried thyme
- Pepper and salt to taste
- ¼ cup of water
- 2 tablespoons of cornstarch

Instructions:

1. Cook your bacon in a large skillet over medium-low heat until it is crisp and then transfer it to paper towels to drain.

2. Once drained, add the bacon to the slow cooker and reheat the skillet with 1 teaspoon of the fat.

3. Add the chicken and cook it for a few minutes on each side until it is browned then place it in the slow cooker.

4. Pour the wine into the skillet and scrape up all the browned bits then transfer it all to the slow cooker.

5. Add in your mushrooms, onions, and garlic along with the rosemary and thyme – season with pepper and salt according to taste.

6. Cover the slow cooker and let everything cook for 5 to 6 hours on the low heat setting until the chicken is cooked through.

7. Use a slotted spoon to remove the chicken, bacon and the vegetables to a serving bowl.

8. Pour the liquid into a saucepan and heat it over medium heat.

9. Whisk together the water and cornstarch to make a slurry and then whisk it into the saucepan – cook for a few minutes until it thickens.

10. Serve the chicken and mushrooms drizzled with the gravy.

Vegetarian Black Bean Butternut Squash Chili

Servings: 6 to 8

Ingredients:

- 1 large butternut squash
- 1 teaspoon of olive oil
- 1 large yellow onion, chopped up
- 2 cloves of garlic, minced
- 1 medium green bell pepper, cored and chopped
- 2 (15-ounce) cans of black beans, rinsed and drained
- 2 (14-ounce) cans of diced tomatoes with juices
- 2 jalapeno peppers, seeded and chopped
- 4 cups of vegetable broth
- 1 ½ tablespoons of chili powder
- 1 ½ teaspoons of ground cumin
- ¼ teaspoon of ground cinnamon
- Pepper and salt to taste

Instructions:

1. Cut your butternut squash in half lengthwise and then scoop out and discard the seeds.
2. Peel away the flesh with a sharp knife and cut the squash into cubes and set aside.
3. Heat up the oil in a large skillet on the medium heat setting.
4. Add your onions and garlic then cook them for 4 to 5 minutes until the onions are translucent.
5. Stir in your bell peppers and cook for another 2 to 3 minutes.
6. Transfer this mixture to your slow cooker and add in the butternut squash, the black beans, the diced tomatoes, and the jalapeno.
7. Stir together your vegetable broth with the chili powder, cumin, and cinnamon then season it all with pepper and salt to taste.
8. Pour the broth mixture into your slow cooker and then cover it with the lid.
9. Let everything cook for 5 to 6 hours on the high heat setting until your squash is tender.
10. Stir it all together and adjust the seasonings, if needed, then serve it hot.

PART 4

Gluten-Free Slow Cooker Snacks and Desserts

Cinnamon Walnut Banana Bread
Servings: 6 to 8

Ingredients:

- Cooking spray
- 1 cup of white granulated sugar
- 1 stick of unsalted butter, melted
- 2 large eggs, whisked well
- 2 cups of all-purpose gluten-free flour
- ¾ teaspoon of baking powder

- ¾ teaspoon of baking soda
- ½ teaspoon of ground cinnamon
- ¼ teaspoon of ground nutmeg
- Pinch of salt
- 3 medium-sized bananas, peeled and mashed up
- ½ cup chopped walnuts

Instructions:

1. Grease the insert for your slow cooker using cooking spray so the bread doesn't stick.
2. In a mixing bowl, combine your sugar and butter with your eggs until well combined.
3. In a separate bowl, whisk together your flour with the baking powder and baking soda.
4. Stir in your cinnamon, nutmeg, and the salt and then whisk all of the dry ingredients into the wet mixture.
5. Fold in your mashed bananas and the walnuts and then pour it all into the slow cooker.
6. Cover your slow cooker with two layers of paper towel and place the lid on top.
7. Let the bread cook for 4 hours on the low setting until it is done in the middle.

Easy Paleo Strawberry Applesauce
Servings: 12 to 16

Ingredients:

- 6 ripe Granny Smith apples
- 2 cups of fresh sliced strawberries
- ½ cup of melted coconut oil
- 1 tablespoons of lemon juice
- 4 to 5 tablespoons of coconut sugar
- 1 teaspoon of ground cinnamon
- 1 teaspoon of vanilla extract

- ½ teaspoon of salt

Instructions:

1. Grease the insert for your slow cooker using cooking spray so the ingredients don't stick.

2. Peel and slice your apples and place them in your slow cooker with the strawberries.

3. In a microwave-safe bowl, melt your coconut oil and then stir in the lemon juice, coconut sugar, cinnamon, vanilla and salt.

4. Pour the mixture over the ingredients in your slow cooker and stir it all together.

5. Cover your slow cooker with the lid and then let the mixture cook for 4 hours on the high heat setting.

6. Turn off the slow cooker and mash the ingredients together using a potato masher or use an immersion blender to puree it.

7. Serve your strawberry applesauce warm or spoon it into jars for storage.

Gluten-Free Chocolate Cake
Servings: 6 to 8

Ingredients:

- 1 cup of gluten-free all-purpose flour
- 6 tablespoons of white granulated sugar
- 4 tablespoons of cocoa powder, divided
- 1 ½ teaspoons of baking powder
- ½ cup of milk (your choice)
- 2 tablespoons of canola oil
- ½ tablespoon of vanilla extract
- ¾ cups of light brown sugar, packed well
- 1 ½ cups of boiling hot water

Instructions:

1. Grease the insert for your slow cooker using cooking spray so the cake doesn't stick.
2. In a mixing bowl, combine your flour and sugar together with 2 tablespoons cocoa powder and the baking powder until well combined.

3. Stir in your milk along with the oil and the vanilla extract until smooth.

4. Fold in your chocolate chips and walnuts (if using) and then pour it all into the slow cooker.

5. In another bowl, whisk together your brown sugar and the rest of the cocoa powder with the boiling water until it forms a smooth sauce.

6. Pour the chocolate sauce over the ingredients in your slow cooker.

7. Cover your slow cooker with a layer of paper towel and place the lid on top.

8. Let the cake cook for 2 hours on the high setting until it is done in the middle.

9. Turn off your slow cooker and let your cake cool for ½ hour before you serve it.

Paleo Spiced Pumpkin Custard
Servings: 4 to 6

Ingredients:

- Water, as needed
- 2 (15-ounce) cans of pumpkin puree
- 6 large eggs, whisked well
- ¼ cup of canned coconut milk
- ¼ cup of honey or pure maple syrup
- 2 tablespoons of coconut oil
- 3 teaspoons of pumpkin pie spice
- ½ tablespoons of vanilla extract
- Pinch of salt

Instructions:

1. Fill your slow cooker with enough water that it comes about 1 inch up the sides.
2. Cover your slow cooker with the lid and then turn it on to high heat and let it warm up for about 45 minutes.
3. Empty your cans of pumpkin into a blender then add in your eggs, coconut milk and honey.

4.   Add in your coconut oil, pumpkin pie spice, and the vanilla extract then add a pinch of salt.

5.   Blend it all up until it is very smooth and completely combined.

6.   Pour the blended mixture into ramekins or custard cups and place them in the slow cooker – do not fill them more than 2/3 full.

7.   Cover your slow cooker and steam the custards on the high heat setting for 5 hours.

8.   Turn off the slow cooker and let the custards cool for a little while before you serve them.

Vegan Walnut Cranberry Stuffed Apples
Servings: 6

Ingredients:

- 6 ripe apples (your choice)
- ¾ cups of coconut butter
- 4 to 6 tablespoons of almond butter
- 2 tablespoons of ground cinnamon
- ¼ teaspoon of salt
- ¼ cup of dried cranberries, chopped

- ¼ cup of chopped walnuts
- ¼ cup of unsweetened shredded coconut
- Apple juice or water, as needed

Instructions:

1. Use a sharp knife to cut out the core of the apples from the top – leave as much of the apple intact as you can.
2. Melt together your coconut butter and almond butter in the microwave in a microwave-safe bowl.
3. Stir in your cinnamon and salt along with the cranberries, walnuts, and shredded coconut.
4. Spoon that mixture into your cored apples and then place them upright in your slow cooker.
5. Pour a little bit of apple juice or water into the slow cooker so the bottom is not dry.
6. Cover your slow cooker with the lid and then cook the apples for 2 to 3 hours on the low heat setting until they are tender.

Cinnamon Apple Crisp
Servings: 6 to 8

Apple **Ingredients:**

- 6 ripe Granny Smith apples
- 2 tablespoons of lemon juice
- ¼ cup of white granulated sugar
- 1 ¼ teaspoon of ground cinnamon
- ½ teaspoon of baking powder
- 1 teaspoon of vanilla extract

Topping **Ingredients:**

- ½ cup of old-fashioned oats (gluten-free)
- ½ cup of gluten-free all-purpose flour blend
- ½ cup of white granulated sugar
- ½ cup of light brown sugar
- 1 teaspoon of ground cinnamon
- ½ teaspoon of ground nutmeg
- ¼ teaspoon of salt
- 1 stick of unsalted butter, chopped

Instructions:

1. Grease the insert for your slow cooker using cooking spray so the ingredients don't stick.

2. Slice up your apples and put them in your slow cooker then toss in the lemon juice.

3. Sprinkle in the white sugar, cinnamon and baking powder then stir it all up with the vanilla extract.

4. To make the topping, toss together your oats and flour with the two sugars as well as the cinnamon, nutmeg and the salt.

5. Cut in the softened butter using a pastry cutter to create a crumbled topping.

6. Spread this crumbled topping over your apple mixture and then cover your slow cooker with the lid.

7. Cook the apple crisp mixture on the low heat setting for 4 hours until it is hot and bubbling – lift the lid a little during the last hour so it becomes crispy.

8. Serve your apple crisp hot with vanilla ice cream.

Spiced Blueberry Coffee Cake
Servings: 8 to 10

Ingredients:

- 1 ¾ cups of gluten-free baking mix, divided
- ¼ cup of light brown sugar, packed
- 1 teaspoon of ground cinnamon
- ¾ cups of white granulated sugar
- ½ cup of plain Greek yogurt

- 1 large egg, whisked well
- 1 teaspoon of vanilla extract
- 1 to ½ cups of fresh blueberries

Instructions:

1. Line the bottom of your slow cooker with parchment paper and then grease it using cooking spray so the ingredients don't stick.
2. Combine together ¼ cup of baking mix, brown sugar and cinnamon in a bowl until it forms a crumbled mixture and then set it aside.
3. In another bowl, combine the rest of the baking mix with the white sugar, yogurt, egg and vanilla extract until it is smooth and combined.
4. Pour about half of the batter into the slow cooker and spread it out evenly.
5. Sprinkle about half of the crumbled mixture and half of the blueberries over top.
6. Spread the rest of the batter on top and finish it off with the rest of the crumbled mixture and the blueberries.
7. Cover your slow cooker with the lid and let it cook for 1 ½ to 2 hours until the middle of the cake is cooked through.

8.   Let the cake cool for about 10 minutes and then lift it out of the slow cooker using the parchment paper.

Vegan Cranberry Orange Poached Pears
Servings: 6

Ingredients:

- 4 cups of unsweetened cranberry juice
- 2 cups of unsweetened orange juice
- 2 tablespoons of fresh orange zest
- 2 to 3 cinnamon sticks
- 6 ripe medium-sized pears
- 2 tablespoons of cornstarch

Instructions:

1. Combine the cranberry juice, orange juice and orange zest in your slow cooker then add the cinnamon sticks.
2. Peel your pears and place them upright in the slow cooker.
3. Cover your slow cooker with the lid and cook the pears for 3 to 4 hours on the low heat setting – you may need to turn them occasionally.
4. Spoon out about ½ cup of the liquid from the slow cooker and whisk in the cornstarch.

5.   Remove the pears and cinnamon sticks from the slow cooker and stir in the cornstarch mixture.

6.   Cook the liquid on the high heat setting with the lid removed until it thickens into a syrup.

7.   Serve the pears in small bowls drizzled with the syrup.

Easy Lemon Blueberry Dump Cake
Servings: 10 to 12

Ingredients:

- Cooking spray
- 2 (21-ounce) cans of blueberry pie filling
- ¼ cup of fresh lemon juice
- 2 tablespoons of fresh lemon zest
- 1 box of gluten-free yellow or white cake mix
- 1 stick of unsalted butter, melted

Instructions:

1. Grease the insert for your slow cooker using cooking spray so the ingredients don't stick.
2. Empty your cans of blueberry pie filling into your slow cooker and stir in the lemon juice and the lemon zest.
3. In a mixing bowl stir together your cake mix and the melted butter.
4. Spread the cake mixture over your blueberry pie filling and then cover the slow cooker with the lid.

5.   Let the mixture cook on the high heat setting for 2 hours or on the low setting for 4 hours.

6.   Remove the lid from the slow cooker and let the cake cool for about 20 minutes before you serve it.

Paleo Vegan Pumpkin Pie Pudding
Servings: 6 to 8

Ingredients:

- 2 (15-ounce) cans of pumpkin puree
- 2 ¼ cups of canned coconut milk
- 3 large eggs, whisked well
- 3 tablespoons of coconut flour
- 2 tablespoons of vanilla extract
- 1 teaspoon of ground cinnamon

- ½ teaspoon of ground nutmeg

- ¼ teaspoon of ground allspice

- Pinch of salt

- 1 teaspoon of baking powder

- Dried fruit, to serve

- Chopped nuts, to serve

Instructions:

1. Grease the insert for your slow cooker using cooking spray so the ingredients don't stick.

2. Empty your cans of pumpkin into the slow cooker and then stir in your coconut milk and eggs.

3. Add the maple syrup along with the coconut flour, vanilla extract, spices, and baking powder.

4. Whisk it all together until it is perfectly smooth and well combined.

5. Cover the slow cooker with the lid and let the pudding cook for 6 to 8 hours on the low heat setting until it is thickened – it will form a crust on the top.

6. Spoon the pudding into bowls and serve with dried fruit and chopped nuts.

Before you go, I'd like to remind you that there is a free, complimentary eBook waiting for you. Download it today to treat yourself to healthy, <u>gluten-free desserts and snacks</u> so that you never feel deprived again!

Download link

<u>http://bit.ly/gluten-free-desserts-book</u>

Conclusion

While the gluten-free diet is a medical treatment for individuals with celiac disease or gluten intolerance, it can be beneficial for nearly everyone. Before you decide whether the gluten-free diet is the right choice for you, take the time to learn as much as you can about the diet including its benefits, its risks, and which foods you can and cannot eat. Check out my website for more information where you will find the food lists and recipes to get started:

http://www.kiraglutenfreerecipes.com

My main focus, as an author, is to create helpful and information gluten-free and anti-inflammatory recipe books that can accommodate vegans, vegetarians and paleo diet enthusiasts.

To post an honest review

One more thing… If you have received any value from this book, can you please rank it and post a short review? It only takes a few seconds really and it would really make my day. It's you I am writing for and your opinion is always much appreciated. In order to do so;

- Log into your account
- Search for my book on Amazon or check your orders/ or go to my author page at:

http://amazon.com/author/kira-novac

- Click on a book you have read, then click on "reviews" and "create your review".

Please let me know your favorite motivational tip you learned from this book.

I would love to hear from you!

If you happen to have any questions or doubts about this book, please e-mail me at:

kira.novac@kiraglutenfreerecipes.com

I am here to help!

Recommended Reading

Book Link:

http://bit.ly/gluten-free-beginners-book

Recommended Reading

Book Link:

http://bit.ly/vegan-spiralizer

FOR MORE HEALTH BOOKS (KINDLE & PAPERBACK) BY KIRA NOVAC PLEASE VISIT:

www.kiraglutenfreerecipes.com/books

Thank you for taking an interest in my work,

Kira and Holistic Wellness Books

HOLISTIC WELLNESS & HEALTH BOOKS

If you are interested in health, wellness, spirituality and personal development, visit our page and be the first one to know about free and 0.99 eBooks:

www.HolisticWellnessBooks.com

Made in the USA
Columbia, SC
12 January 2018